Query Letter Swipe File:

Exact Words, Phrases and Templates to Write Query Letters, Get Literary Agents and Publish Books for Life

By Christopher Kokoski

D1501686

Author: Christopher Kokoski

Beta Readers: John R. Kokoski

Book Cover Designer: www.ebooklaunch.com

If you need editing services, please consider www.Volo-Press.com

For my children, Lilly and Grayson. I love you to the moon. You surprise, amaze, delight and humble me every day. See you on the dream train…

FREE GIFT!

DOWNLOAD YOUR BONUSES NOW

If you are reading the print version or listening to the audio version, please type the following url into your Internet browser:

http://www.subscribepage.com/InsideSwipeFileBook

TABLE OF CONTENTS

INTRODUCTION

Query Letter: A query letter is a short, one-page letter that sells you and your novel to a literary agent. Agents then connect authors with book publishers.

Swipe File: A secret file top professionals keep of their most used, recommended, tested and proven tactics for ultimate success in their trade.

Note: This is a swipe file for fiction only.

I landed an agent with my very first query letter.

How? For the last 20+ years, I've been obsessed with excavating **the hidden patterns, forces and shortcuts that dramatically accelerate positive responses from literary agents and publishers**.

I've spent thousands of hours pouring over books, articles, reports, tip sheets and attending webinars and workshops on writing query letters. I've studied literal hundreds of successful query letters.

With this insider knowledge, you can easily get requests for sample chapters, manuscripts and offers for full representation. I can help you get them all; and, yes, you can get them with your VERY FIRST QUERY.

How? By applying the very same tactics and strategies I used to get an agent with *my* very first query letter.

Other books on writing query letters tell you WHAT to do with endless lists, vague pointers, hints and explanations that stop short of giving you the tools of HOW to actually put your words on paper.

This is not one of those books.

This is all actionable content – the exact words and phrases and templates that you can put into immediate use in your own letters.

In other words, **this book doesn't just tell you what to do; it virtually does it for you**. In this short book, you'll find more than theory – you'll get the secret swipe file of bestselling authors, literary agents and big publishing houses.

Imagine a crowd of publishing experts looking over your shoulder and feeding you the specific language to use to get them to say, "YES!" Imagine never staring at a blank page again without a clue of how to sum up your novel into a concise one-page letter. Imagine submitting your query letter with confidence, knowing that it will work.

You are about to step into a virtual vault of bestseller templates with copy-and-paste prompts that leave nothing to chance.

Here's a small sample of what you will get:

- Complete categorized swipe files of irresistible introductions, pitches, book details, bios and salutations that sell stories
- Full paint-by-numbers query templates (it's so easy, my 11-year old wrote a mouth-watering query in less than an hour!)
- Over 100 hypnotic words, magnetic phrases and mind bending lines so that you never run out of options

If you can copy and paste, you can write brilliant query letters that sell your book, novel or series.

I could have written a 300-page book crammed with fluff you don't need to know. I could have priced it at $20 or $30. That's not me. I'm like you: Just a passionate writer who, for once, wants to finally even the playing field.

This book is crammed with the insider information I wish I had when I first started writing query letters. Now it's yours.

Do let me know how it goes for you.

How to Use This Book

You can use this book in three ways:

1. Write your query letter by combining the mother lode of words, phrases and templates provided in this book.
2. Use one of the full query templates in the back of the book.
3. Write your query from scratch and then use this book as a high-caliber revision tool by adding the swipe files to your letter during the editing phase.

To write your query letter in record time, follow the Quick Start Guide below. I will walk you step-by-step through a proven (and simple) strategy to write an irresistible query letter.

Quick Start Guide

Here is how the Quick Start Method works:

Fastest Method

1. Read this entire book all the way through at least once
2. Choose a fully organized and written proven query template (you get 5 to choose from!)
3. Insert your book details into the template (easy peasy)
4. Submit to agents & publishers!

Second Fastest Method

1. Read this entire book all the way through at least once
2. Choose words, phrases and sentence templates from each section (Hook, Pitch, Book Details, Bio, Salutation) that most relate to your book or story

3. Organize your words, phrases and sentences into a standard query structure (Hook, Pitch, Book Details, Bio, Salutation)
4. Insert your book details, as needed
5. Submit to agents & publishers!

How to Choose the Perfect Words, Phrases and Sentence Templates for Your Query

Although categorized and selectively grouped into sub-swipe files, almost **any of these words and phrases can work in any genre**. They are *genre-fluid*. The question is: how do you choose which words, phrases and templates are best suited for your story?

Here are few considerations:

1. Consider genre (some words and phrases make more sense in a Romance query than a Horror query)
2. Consider subgenre
3. Consider the words, phrases and templates that best fit YOUR story (characters, conflict, setting, etc.).
   - Who are the characters in your story? What are they like?
   - What is the main conflict in your story?
   - What are other conflicts?
   - What is the main goal in your story?
   - What are the stakes in the story?
   - Are there any ticking clocks in your story?
4. Consider words, phrases and templates that highlight your story's strengths (What's most compelling – your characters, plot, setting, dialogue, etc.?)

How to Fill in The Blanks

In this book, you will find tons of individual words that you can drop into any sentence or phrase. You'll also find groups of words or phrases that you can use verbatim or drop into any relevant sentence that you craft. <u>The phrases come in a variety of forms: a starting phrase, middle phrase or end phrase. Other times, you'll find full sentences.</u> Phrases with gender specific pronouns like "she" or "he" can easily be replaced to fit your story. Finally, you'll find phrases and sentences that include brackets with placeholder recommendations – [TITLE], [CHARACTER] – into which you can insert your story details.

What Story Details to Insert In the Bracketed Template Phrases

- Character names (first name, last name, full name or nickname)
- Main plot points
- Crises or inciting event
- Conflict (this is used to cover a broad scope of problems, trouble, tension, threats, obstacles, antagonists, or any person or force that prevents the protagonist(s) from reaching their goals)
- Goals, including the main story goal
- Setting or world of your story (Africa, FBI, Outer Space, etc.)
- Time (day, week, month)
- Word count
- Your book title (written in ALL CAPS)
- The genre of your book
- Bestselling authors in your genre
- Bestseller books in your genre similar to your story (italicized)
- Personal details about an agent (what genre they represent, their favorite type of stories, their blogs, social media, etc.)

By the way, it's helpful to have certain information on hand when writing your query letter. Collect key information (title, character names, word count, etc.) prior to writing your query letter and you'll maximize the *Query Letter Swipe File*. I recommend organizing the data into a one-page list for easy accessibility.

Here is a list of popular genres as a starting point:

- Action/Adventure
- Erotica
- Fantasy
- Horror
- Literary Fiction
- Mystery
- Thriller/Suspense
- Romance
- Sci-fi
- Westerns
- Women's fiction
- Young Adult/New Adult/Middle Grade

Note: This is not an all-encompassing list and there are many subgenres to further define stories.

If you Google "How do I know the genre for my story?", you will find lots of great free blog posts and articles to help you define the genre and subgenre of your particular story.

Most writing software includes features to track word count. For example, in the current version of Microsoft Word, you can figure out your word count by opening your manuscript, going to Tools and clicking on Word Count.

Freedom of the Muse (And Doing the Impossible)

While this book provides a virtual paint-by-numbers approach, no book can cover every detail of your specific story. That would take an entire library just to make an honest attempt.

In other words, it's impossible.

However, this book comes closest to the ideal query guide by providing precise language and sentence templates for you to describe your specific story. While you will likely run into occasional gaps between the material in this book and describing the fine details of your story, use these templates to jumpstart your muse. This resource is like no other and it's my privilege to share it with you.

Additional Tips on Writing a Killer Query Letter

- Embrace query letters as professional sales letters (it's a helpful mental filter for thinking about and writing query letters that win)
- Keep your letter to one single-spaced page.
- Be concise (shoot for 3-5 paragraphs, 200-500 words total)
- Write the Pitch section in present tense (She discovers, he goes on the run, etc.)
- Use active language (jump, triggers, races ahead)
- Use emotional language (devastated, heartbroken, overwhelmed)
- Use specific language ("25-year old" instead of "young", "Ex-cop" instead of "law enforcement experience")
- Focus on contrast & juxtaposition (fall in love - but the person is dead, a gift brings a blessing but comes at an unthinkable cost)

Standard Query Structure

As a way of organizing this book, I decided to follow the most popular structure of effective query letters. There are multiple variations of this structure – I discovered at least 6 in my research – but this standard outline will serve as a guiding framework as we move forward.

Here is the standard query structure:

Dear [Literary Agent Name],

Hook – Grab Attention or Introduction

Pitch – Lay out your story (characters, setting, goals, conflict, story stakes, ticking clock)

Book Details – Genre, word count, book comparisons, book series, etc.

Bio (optional) – Awards, platform, expertise, experience

Salutation – What's included with the letter (sample chapters, synopsis, etc.), thanks and goodbye

[Author Name]

Again, this is a standard structure that includes all the elements of a professional query letter. That's another way of saying: You could write every query letter in this structure and literary agents would love you for it.

What to Expect

From this point forward, we will start with the swipe file for hooks and then work our way through each section of successful query letters. For the Hook and Pitch sections, we'll drill even deeper into sub-swipe files. It'll all be categorized for easy access when you go to write your very own successful query letter.

We'll finish up with a set of complete query templates you can use as is or tweak to your personal specifications. The only real rule in writing queries is that it has to work.

Welcome to what works.

SECTION 1: HOOK SWIPE FILE

This first swipe file section shows you exactly how to start your query letter so that agents can't put it down. It's called the Hook Swipe File because its main purpose is to hook an agent's attention fast and propel them through the rest of your letter.

The hook is the most important part of your query letter. Why? If your letter doesn't immediately grab attention, an agent or publisher is unlikely to even *read* the rest of your letter.

So, in this section, you'll learn the exact words, phrases and sentence templates to hook agents from line one.

Note that a hook may contain information also covered in the Book Detail Swipe File Section, information such as your book title, genre and word count. While I've saved most of those templates for the Book Details Swipe File Section, I have included samples here as well. Some authors choose to put this book information upfront, while others save it for near the end of the query. The choice is up to you. Either option is present in many successful query letters. However, only choose one spot. There is no need to repeat this information in a single letter.

For your convenience, I have categorized the hooks into several sub-swipe files:

- Connection
- Direct Introduction
- Hook Statement/Mini-Pitch
- Question

In a *Connection* hook, you (ideally) remind an agent of how you know each other or you personalize the query by showing that you have done your research on the agent. A *Direct*

Introduction hook is just that: plainly stating your purpose for writing the query letter, a.k.a. to get representation. The *Hook Statement/Mini-Pitch* is typically one sentence or a short series of phrases that serve as a compact summary of the entire story, sort of like a tag line for a movie. The Question hook is starting with a question – usually blurring the lines with the Mini-Pitch.

Connection

[TITLE OF BOOK THE AGENT REPRESENTS] has been both an inspiration and teaching aid.

[NAME OF REFERRING PROFESSIONAL CONTACT] referred me to you.

[WELL-KNOWN EDITOR, AGENT, AGENT CLIENT, MUTUAL FRIEND] referred me to you and your agency.

As a faithful reader of your blog...

As a subscriber to your podcast...

As a subscriber to your YouTube channel...

As you represent strong authors in the [GENRE] genre...

Because

Because you represent [GENRE] like [BESTSELLER TITLE] by [BESTSELLING AUTHOR]

Congratulations on your recent new position at...

Due to your expressed interest in quality [GENRE] fiction, I think my novel, [TITLE], would be perfect for you

Due to your interest in...I thought you would be a perfect fit for [TITLE].

Given your enthusiasm for...

Given your interest in [GENRE], I thought it might be a good fit for your list.

I am writing in response to your request at/on [LOCATION or CONFERENCE]

I appreciate your approach to agent-client relationships

I enjoyed [PERSONAL DETAILS ABOUT AGENT – BLOG, WEBINAR, etc.]. Because of this, I'd love for you to consider my [GENRE] novel, [TITLE]

I enjoyed [PERSONAL DETAILS ABOUT AGENTS]. Because of this, I'd love for you to consider my [GENRE] novel, [TITLE]

I enjoyed your interview…

I have followed your blog with interest

I have specifically chosen you because...

I loved [BOOK AGENT REPRESENTS]

I noticed on Twitter…

I noticed on your Publisher's Marketplace page that you represent quite a few [GENRE] novels

I read in an interview that...As such, I thought you might like...

I read on your site that your agency is currently looking for stories with…

I recently saw the sale announcement for [MAJOR BOOK PUBLISHING DEAL OF THEIRS]

I understand you are a fan of both [GENRE] and [GENRE], and therefore believe your agency would be a great fit.

I was thrilled to read your tweet yesterday stating that you love [ENTER THEME, CHARACTERS, BOOK DETAILS THAT MATCH YOUR NOVEL].

I would love to work with you, and I hope you'll be interested in my [GENRE] novel, [TITLE]

I'm contacting you personally because of your stellar reputation

If my name looks familiar...

I'm sending this to you because of your request for "[QUOTE THEIR WORDS VERBATIM]"

I've followed your [SOCIAL MEDIA ACCOUNT, BLOG, PODCAST] for a long time and I find it very helpful

I've long dreamed of querying you...

I've since enjoyed your words on...

Knowing you are a fan of...

Thank you so much for agreeing to take a look at my manuscript, [TITLE].

Thanks so much for...

We met at...

We recently met at...

When I learned that you represent...

When I saw your listing in Writer's Marketplace, and that you represented [BESTSELLING AUTHOR'S NAME] and her/his book, [BOOK TITLE], I knew I wanted to send you my...

When I saw your listing in Writer's Marketplace, I knew I wanted to send you my...

When we met at the [CONFERENCE or EVENT] in [MONTH]...

You and I... [MET AT/SHARED A TWITTER CONVERSATION, etc]

You've mentioned your interest in representing novels with...

Special circumstance: Resubmitting your Query Letter

"After taking into careful consideration the feedback I was given by [NAME OF AGENT OR EDITOR] of your agency, I would like to resubmit my query..."

Special Circumstance: Twitter #Pitmad

Thank you for liking my #Pitmad tweet "[PITMAD TWEET FROM TWITTER]."

(Note: #Pitmad is a Twitter pitch event where authors tweet a story premise and interested agents respond)

Direct Introduction

80,000-word contemporary romance

96,000-word thriller with paranormal elements

As a [YEAR] [PRESTIGOUS NATIONAL CONTEST] finalist, I am seeking representation for my novel [TITLE].

Complete at 93,000 words

I am submitting my...

I am currently seeking representation...

I am hoping you will be interested in my [GENRE] titled [TITLE], complete at [WORD COUNT] words.

I am seeking representation for...

I am seeking new representation because my former agent...

I am writing to…

I'm writing to seek representation for my [WORD COUNT]-word [GENRE].

I'm writing to see if you might be interested in working with me and my [GENRE] novel, [TITLE]

I would like to present my [GENRE] novel for your consideration.

I'd like to tell you about my [GENRE] novel…

I'd like to tell you about my novel, [BOOK TITLE]

Please consider representing my [GENRE] novel, [TITLE OF YOUR BOOK].

Hook Statement/Mini-Pitch

You can start your query letter with a premise or hook statement. That is to say, a one-line pitch statement related to your longer pitch. You will find all the words, phrases and templates for a perfect pitch in the next section.

However, here are a few templates for a compelling hook or premise statement:

[AGE]-year-old [CHARACTER NAME] has never [MUNDANE OR EXPECTED ACTIVITY – BEEN OUTSIDE, KNOWN LOVE, SEEN ANOTHER HUMAN BEING, etc.]

[CHARACTER] has never met a [PERSON, ROLE, EXPERIENCE, MAN, WOMAN, CONFLICT] that was more exciting than a [PERSON, ROLE, EXPERIENCE, CONFLICT, CAREER, SURPRISING HOBBY].

[CHARACTER] may be [GOAL] – if [CHARACTERS] can [GOAL].

[CHARACTERS] were supposed to be [EXTINCT/DEAD].

[CONFLICT/PROBLEM/CRISES] all the time in [SETTING] –

but usually not [CHARACTERS/ROLE/CONTRADICTORY EXPERIENCE].

First [COMMON EXPERIENCE]. First [ANOTHER COMMON EXPERIENCE]. First...[VERY UNCOMMON EXPERIENCE].

It's happening again.

Some [CHARACTERS/ROLE/GROUP] can [ACTION]. [CHARACTER] can [EXTENDED ACTION, MORE THAN WHAT MOST OTHERS CAN DO].

There are few novels written about... and fewer still that focus on...

There's no feeling quite so thrilling as...

This is not a [GENRE] story

[WORD], [WORD], [WORD] aren't just...

And two of my all-time favorite examples:

- Lucifer's youngest son, Jinx, is a failure as a demon (from the query for *D'Evil Diaries* by Tatum Flynn)
- Mankind has finally reached perfection — but she comes at a terrible cost (from the query for *Perfectly Pia* by JNKhoury)

She, indeed.

Question

Have you ever felt like...?

How far would you go to [PROTAGONIST'S GOAL]?

How far would you go to get revenge against your [CHARACTER, ROLE]'s murder?

How many...?

Think that...?

What happens when...?

What if [CRISES, INCITING EVENT OR MAJOR STORY CONFLICT]?

What if the only person you could see yourself with is [PROBLEM or CONFLICT]?

What kind...?

Which...?

SECTION 2:
PITCH SWIPE FILE

The Pitch is the heart and soul of your query. While the hook is the most important section of a query for getting the letter read, the pitch is the most critical part for getting your story represented. If you get the pitch right, an agent will often overlook many other imperfections in your query.

Most of the time, your pitch will be paragraph 1 or 2 of your letter.

The purpose of the pitch is to concisely sum up your story (main characters, main conflict, main goals, main setting, story stakes/consequences and ticking clocks/deadlines).

I explain the essential elements of a pitch in more depth in my companion book *How To Get An Agent With Your Very First Query* **(Coming in 2018)**

However, for now, I want you to focus on laying out the main points of your story using the words, phrases and template sentences in this swipe file. Many wield power alone, but the real magic happens when you combine several together.

A helpful framework for writing a pitch is: Character + Goal + Conflict + Story Stakes + Ticking Clocks. If you write a paragraph or two about something terrible happening to someone, why it matters and how long they have to fix it, then you will be well on your way to penning a perfect query letter.

While this swipe file section is divided into multiple sub-swipe files (character, conflict, setting, etc.), please note that these swipe files are generally combined when writing your actual query letter. The separate categories in this book are for clarity and instructional purposes only.

Please note that the Conflict category is broad, combining conflict of all shapes and sizes. Conflict can mean any problem, threat or complication. It might refer to the core conflict of the story or a side conflict that spirals off the core. It can mean external or internal conflict, and sometimes both.

The Compelling Phrases, Questions, Power Words and Transition Words swipe files can be dropped into any part of your pitch (and sometimes even other sections of your letter, if appropriate). The Compelling Phrases and Power Words can be used to start or end sentences, frame a story premise, introduce a character or conflict, or as a transition within the pitch section.

Read through this section, select phrases from each category, and then mix and match them until they click with your story. If you have any questions, don't worry: you'll get a set of full query letter templates at the end of the book.

Character

[AGE] + [CHARACTER] is a professional [PROFESSION – ACTUAL OR MADE UP]

[AGE] + [CHARACTER] has the [POSITIVE TRAIT], [POSITIVE TRAIT] and [POSITIVE TRAIT] that make him the envy of the [SETTING]

[AGE] + [CHARACTER] would take [UNIQUE CHARACTER PREFERENCE] over [COMMON PREFERENCE] any day.

[AGE+ JOB or ROLE] + [CHARACTER NAME]

[CHARACTER ROLE] + [CHARACTER] isn't normal... so when he...

[CHARACTER TRAIT OR SPECIAL GIFT, POWER] comes easily to [CHARACTER]

[CHARACTER TRAIT] + [ROLE] + [CHARACTER NAME] is [TIME FRAME] from [FINISHING, COMPLETING, GOAL]

[CHARACTER] and [CHARACTER] are drawn to each other

[CHARACTER] barely survived the [CONFLICT] that left her…

[CHARACTER] Can't…but she can…

[CHARACTER] finds sanctuary with…

[CHARACTER] had been [ROLE/CAREER, POSITION], before…

[CHARACTER] has [GREAT ACHIEVEMENTS, FAME, etc.], but now [COMPLETE OPPOSITE/MUNDANE]

[CHARACTER] has a secret he'd kill to keep quiet

[CHARACTER] has always prided herself on…

[CHARACTER] has been waiting his whole life for…

[CHARACTER] has everything she wants: [EXAMPLE], [EXAMPLE] and [EXAMPLE].

[CHARACTER] has fallen from [ROLE, STATUS] to [ROLE, STATUS]

[CHARACTER] has lost everything

[CHARACTER] has never met a woman more interesting than…

[CHARACTER] has secrets of his own to keep

[CHARACTER] has spent her whole life believing…

[CHARACTER] has…but now…

[CHARACTER] is able to…

[CHARACTER] is not a…

[CHARACTER] is smart, attractive and…

[CHARACTER] is the top…

[CHARACTER] isn't the only [STATUS/POSITION] in town

[CHARACTER] isn't like other [ROLE]

[CHARACTER] struggles to reclaim…

[CHARACTER] was born to be a…

[CHARACTER] will never…

[CHARACTER] wonders what it is about him that makes [CONFLICT/PROBLEM/PAIN]

[CHARACTER]'s world is divided by...

[SITUATION] + [ROLE]

[TITLE] introduces [CHARACTER], a [ADJECTIVE] and [ACJECTIVE] + [AGE] + [ROLE] who's facing [CONFLICT/CRISES].

15-year old…

27-year-old [CHARACTER], [NICKNAME]...

A [CHARACTER ROLE, JOB/POSITION] with the ability to…

A deadly combination of…

A force to be reckoned with

A once...he now...

Adrenaline-junkie

Adrenaline-pumping career as…

Agent

Aided by…

All [CHARACTER] has left is…

Alpha

As much as [CHARACTER] would like to believe...

Ashamed of…

Bad boy

Beauty queen

Becoming the first…

Best friend

Beta

Born in a…

Brilliant

Burdened by...

Businessman

But [CHARACTER AGE] + [CHARACTER NAME] has a secret: she wants [SECRET].

But [CHARACTER] is fed up with…

But [CHARACTER]'s [POSITIVE TRAIT] proves stronger than [OPPOSTIVE TRAIT]

But most [AGE]-year old [ROLE/STATUS/POSITION] don't…

But when…he must…

Career as…

CEO

Cheerful

Cocky

Competitor

Damaged

Daughter of…

Deep wounds

Demon

Despite their past...

Devilish

Disfigured

Disgraced

Dog walker

Driven by…

Ekes out a living

Elite

Elite soldier

Enlisting the aid of…

Enter [CHARACTER NAME]

Estranged

Even [CHARACTERS] get involved

Ex- [POLICE OFFICER/LAWYER/SPECIAL OPS, etc.]

Ex-CIA

Failed astronaut

Fairy

Feels like normal life is in reach

Fiancé

First love

Flirt

For 18 -year-old…

Forced together

Gets help from…

Ghost

Gifted

Girl-next-door

Good looks

Guardian

He has a destiny – [DESTINY/GOAL]

He is torn between…

He isn't just…he is also…

He wants nothing to do with…

He's too clever to…

Her days are…until she meets...

Her gift allows her to... but leaves her...

Hiding secrets of her own

His life revolves around…

Horse whisperer

Hot shot

Husband

Icy

In private…In public…

Independent

Italian family

Legend

Living among…

Loner

Maidens

Master assassin

Mercenary

Mild-mannered

Military

Misfit

Monster

Most [ATTRIBUTE/CHARACTER DESCRIPTION]

NYPD Detective

Of all the [ROLE/POSITION/STATUS] …

Office drone

Old flame

Old friend

Only one who can...

Outran his tragic past

Party girl

Physicist

Polish heritage

Preppy

Prisoner

Prodigy

Promising future

Queen

Raised by...

Raised in...

Raised to believe…

Reformed

Reluctant

Retired CIA agent

Retired…

Rival

Rough around the edges

Rugged

Sadistic

Sassy

Scarred by…

Seasoned pro

Second in command…

Self-absorbed

Seventeen-year-old

Sexy

Shadowy past

She is the only one who knows...

She is the only one who may be able to prevent...

She was [AGE] years old when he first...

Single mother

Smart [CHARACTER ROLE] know to avoid...

Son of...

Special

Spitfire

Still haunted by...

Still reeling from...

Striking

Struggles to cope

Superhuman

Swore he'd never return

Sworn to kill

The last thing she is looking for is a serious relationship

Then, a week before...[CONFLICT].

To all appearances...

Troll

Two unlikely companions

Type-A

Tyrant

Ugly secret [CHARACTER] never wanted anyone to know

Unlikely adversary

Unsatisfied with…

Unwilling

Upbringing in…

Uptight

Violent

War criminal

Wealthy elite

When you're [ROLE/STATUS], you [BLESSING, CURSE, PROBLEM, CONFLICT or RESULT]

While other [CHARACTERS LIKE YOUR PROTAGONIST, ROLE, STATUS] dream about [COMMON DREAMS OR GOALS FOR THIS GROUP], all [PROTAGONIST] dreams about is…

Wife

With only a [CHARACTER] with [CONFLICT/PROBLEM] for company

With the exception of…

With the help of…

Witness

Young

Compelling Phrases

[CHARACTER] has other ideas

[CHARACTER] is not about to…

[CHARACTER] must find the strength within himself

[CHARACTER] suspects the [ITEM, PERSON, SETTING] might be more than just a…

[CHARACTER] was supposed to be...

[NUMBER OF] weeks before…

[NUMBER] of years in the making

[UNCONVENTIONAL CONCEPT, TRAIT, EXPERIENCE] is as conventional as [CONVENTIONAL CONCEPT, TRAIT, EXPERIENCE]

A far cry from…

A friendship that neither expected

A man from his past

A modern day…

A night full of [ACTION/EXPERIENCES, etc] lands him in…

About to change forever

After a lifetime of…

Against all odds

All he has to do is…

All she knows for certain is…

An encounter with...

Ancient evil

Ancient prophesy

And winds up in…

Another blow to…

Arrives uninvited

As he digs deeper…

As long as…

As the story opens…

At first…

At the same time...

Barely scraping by

Before [CHARACTER] knows it…

Before he…

Before it can...

Before it…

Before she can…

Before she…

Before they…

Body count

Break the vow

Breathless for more

Bridge an alliance

Broken heart

Brutal efficiency

Buried memories

Buried secret

Bury the past

But [EMOTION] turns to [ANOTHER EMOTION]

But as…

But it is not until…

But just as…

But not everyone is…

But they aren't…

But this year...

But to [CHARACTER]'s surprise…

By day…by night…

Can't afford to…

Carefully laid plans

Center of attention

Chain of events

Chance encounter

Choices entwine

Clear his name

Close to home

Complicated by…

Confess her undying love…

Cross boundaries

Dangerous intersection of…

Dangerous pact

Dark memories

Darker magic

Darker than anything she could've ever imagined

Deep wounds

Deep wounds of her own

Develop into…

Didn't see this coming

Disastrous consequences

Discovers there is a whole lot more…

Dives into…

Doesn't know who to trust

Dramas play out against

Drawn to...

Dream job

Dream vacation

Dream wedding

Driven from…

Each will learn…

Ends up dead

Even though she can…

Every day

Every morning

Except for one thing…

Except this time...

Fall guy

Fallen in love

Falling deeper into…

Family secrets

Follow the clues

For days…

For months...

For reasons he can't understand…

Forge a tenuous truce…

Foul play

Freak accident

Fresh start

From his past

From the day…

From their earliest days…to…

Game of cat and mouse

Glimmer of hope

Grind her down

Gruesome reality of…

Gunned down

Harboring secrets

He can't bring himself to…

He certainly doesn't…

He expected…

He has no idea…

He is faced with…

He might also have [CONFLICT/PROBLEM]

He never dreamed…

He quickly goes from [STATUS] to [STATUS]

He retreats into…

He should be thrilled...

Hell-bent on…

Hiding in plain sight

High-stakes

High-stakes game of…

His [WORK/BIOLOGY, etc.] holds the key to...

Horrific crime

If only…

If she's lucky, she…

In a way he could never imagine

In order to…

In the end…

In the wake of...

In the wings

Information leaked

Instead she…

Isn't just a way to [ACTION, EXPERIENCE, TASK, RESULT, GOAL]—it's a [ANOTHER OFTEN OPPOSITE GOAL, TASK, RESULT, CONFLICT]

Isn't what it seems

It all starts with…

It becomes personal

It begins as...

It happens every...

It isn't long before…

It quickly becomes clear that...

It started as…

It was supposed to be...

It's bad enough that…

It's been a year since...

It's more than…

Just beginning

Just in time for…

Just the beginning

Just when…

Knows nothing of…

Last thing she expects

Learn the price of…

Learns that…

Learns the hard way that…

Learns the true meaning of…

Least of their problems

Leave it all behind…

Left behind is…

Lethal consequences

Life is changing

Like never before

Locking lips

Love affair

Love triangle

Might have everything to do with…

Most powerful weapon

Murder trail leads to…

Mysteries swirling around…

Mysterious artifact

Named as the prime suspect

Never suspecting that…

Never thought possible

Now it's personal

Now the only way for…

Oh, and…

Ominous message

On one condition

On the day…

On the night…

On the run

On the surface…

On the verge of…

On top of all this…

One last…

Only to find

Only way out

Or not.

Or worse.

Out of control

Overcome the agony of his past

Playing a dangerous game

Power struggle

Problem is…

Prompted into action

Quest for justice

Questioning his…

Ramp up

Ramp up their efforts

Reaching its boiling point

Realize there's more to…

Reels him in

Reluctant to…

Reverberate across generations

Right out of her nightmares

Running out of time

Scandalous proposal

Secrets of the past

Set in motion

Setting off a chain of events

She had…and…and…

She has no idea…

She isn't counting on...

She never expected…

She turns to…

She's had his share of…

Shifts off balance

Shock her to her very core

Shock waves are rippling through…

Shortly after…

Shrouded in…

Shut down

Skirts the edge of…

Slinks back to…

So when [CHARACTER] is asked to…

Stand up for…

Start to unravel

Strike out alone

Sucked into…

Swearing off…

Swore he'd never return

Take out…

Takes a turn for the…

Takes unexpected turns

That changes when…

That one decision would…

That was before…

That's what happens when…

The case takes a stranger turn

The forefront of…

The last thing she wants is…

The last thing…

The lines between [DYNAMIC] and [DYNAMIC] begin to blur

The link between

There may be one person who…

There's no feeling quite so…

There's no manual for…

There's only one thing more important than…

There's no how-to manual on how to...

They are not the first…

Time to act

Too good to be true

Trail of blood

Turns out to be…

Turns out to be the least of her problems

Turns the tables

Ultimately realize...

Unanswered questions

Uncharted territory

Uncover clues that lead to...

Uncover evidence

Unearth ancient secrets

Unexpected desire

Unlike any she's ever known

Unlike anything he's had before

Unsettling truths

Until a…

Until it…

Until now

Until she uncovers the truth

Until they…

Urgent problem

Violent tendencies

Vowed never to return

Want her dead

Welcomes the chance to…

When an opportunity arises to...

Whisks her off to…

Will he…or…?

World's biggest…

Worst fears

Conflict/Crises/Inciting Event

[CHARACTER NAME]'s life was perfect until…

[CHARACTER ROLE] + [CHARACTER NAME]'s day goes to hell when...

[CHARACTER] + [CRISES]

[CHARACTER] always…so when…

[CHARACTER] becomes [CONFLICT/PROBLEM]

[CHARACTER] becomes the focal point of…

[CHARACTER] becomes the number one target

[CHARACTER]'s carefree existence is turned upside down

[CHARACTER] didn't count on…

[CHARACTER] doesn't believe in…until he…

[CHARACTER] doesn't want to…not that she has a choice.

[CHARACTER] faces her greatest challenge…

[CHARACTER] finds herself in an unusual situation

[CHARACTER] has finally [GOAL, DREAM COME TRUE]. There's one problem: [CONFLICT].

[CHARACTER] has just made the biggest mistake of her life

[CHARACTER] is devastated to lose…

[CHARACTER] is doomed from the moment…

[CHARACTER] is running out of time

[CHARACTER] knows [ANTAGONIST] is coming for him

[CHARACTER] leads a group of [CHARACTERS] into…

[CHARACTER] must decide…

[CHARACTER] must prevent

[CHARACTER] realizes that the one [ROLE, SETTING, EXPERIENCE] he's been so desperate to get away from just might be the one he wants to [EXPERIENCE, KEEP, PROTECT].

[CHARACTER] stalks [ANOTHER CHARACTER], plots [GOAL or CONFLICT], and gets [CONFLICT] in the process

[CHARACTER] tracks down…

[CHARACTER] tries to [GOAL] but…

[CHARACTER] turns to the same [CONFLICT] that threatens his [SETTING or GOAL] in a dangerous attempt to [GOAL].

[CHARACTER]'s dreams are crushed when…

[CHARACTER]'s hunt for [GOAL] has gone horribly wrong and now he's [CONFLICT].

[CONFLICT] has driven…

[CONFLICT] wasn't in the plan

[LIFE/JOB/MARRIAGE] was hard enough before…

[PERSON, ANIMAL, OBJECT, CONFLICT] is the last thing [CHARACTER] needs

A [CONFLICT]. A [CONFLICT]. A [CONFLICT].

A conspiracy that reaches the highest levels of...

A group of…must fight to…in the face of…

A problem? Not until…

Adding to the…

After escaping…

After... [CHARACTER] is about to...

After…

Against his wishes…

Against the advice

Against the backdrop of…

Against the tradition

All [CHARACTER] can recall is…

All leading up to one explosive night when…

Alone with [CHARACTER]…

An impossible [CONFLICT/PROBLEM] that is supposed to…

As [CONFLICT] draws near…he has to…[CONFLICT].

As he struggles to…

As his past catches up with his present…

As revolution brews in…

As the [ANTAGONIST] closes in, the [PROTAGONIST] must…to survive…

As the [CONFLICTS] intensify…

As… she must come to grips with…

Assaulted

Attacked

Ban him from…

Battle for their very lives

Become the next target

Begins to implode

Between [CONFLICT], keeping [CONFLICT, GOAL], fending off [CONFLICT] and avoiding [CONFLICT]…

Biggest mistake of his life

But [CHARACTER] can be [ROLE] or [ROLE], not both.

But [CHARACTER] is wrong

But [CHARACTER] is…

But [NUMBER] years later…

But as…his perfect [LIFE/JOB/MARRIAGE] starts to unravel

But before she can even...

But by now it's too late

But her involvement in [CONFLICT, CONSPIRACY, MURDER INVESTIGATION] changes that, and sends her...

But his goal is sidetracked when...

But it isn't long before...

But just as...

But little do they know...

But not everyone is as eager to...

But now he's...

But the [GOAL, CHOICE, ACTION] comes at a heavy price

But the [SETTING] is...

But the deeper [CHARACTER] digs...

But the trouble has just begun.

But to face...he needs help from...

But when one of them is...they are forced to...

But when their investigation puts them on the trail of...

Called in to investigate

Caught between...

Caught in the middle

Choosing between...

Close on their heels

Complex web of lies

Complicated by...

Confronting the very [PERSON, PLACE, THING] that...

Cover up

Cursed with...

Cut off from...

Dangerous games are being played

Defies his superiors

Deposited into...

Devastating revelation

Disastrous consequences

Discovers she's the only one who can stop [CONFLICT]

Dodging...dealing with...and coming to terms with...

Double life

Drawn into...

Each mysterious...threatens...

Embarking on a harrowing journey

Events take a catastrophic turn

Everyone he...ends up...

Everything is perfect until...

Everywhere he turns...

Except...

Faces...

Faked her death

Far more dangerous than she thought

Fast-forward to…

Fight like hell to…

Finally follows through with their threat

Find themselves once again drawn to...

Finds a body

Finds himself living a life far different than…

Following the trail

For the first time…

Forced to work together

Forced to…

Fourteen-year-old [CHARACTER]'s [FAMILY MEMBER, FRIEND, COLLEAGUE] has warned her…

Fugitive on the run

He [ACTION] only to find…

He can't avoid...

He certainly doesn't…

He finds evidence…

He has no choice but to...

He isn't counting on...[CONFLICT], [CONFLICT] or [CONFLICT]

He makes a rash decision to…

He now finds himself…

He tries to flee but...

He uncovers a secret conspiracy to…

Her fate lies in the hands of a [MONSTER, KILLER, ASSASIN, TERRORIST, etc.]

Her gift comes with…[CONFLICT, FLAW] and [CONFLICT, FLAW]

Her worst fears are confirmed

His [STATUS QUO] is disrupted when…

His brother is one of those who has been taken.

His deeper look into…reveals disturbing secrets…

His gift comes with a dangerous downside: [DOWNSIDE, CONFLICT]

His only [FRIEND, NEIGHBOR, ALLY] is…

Holds darker secrets

How can he fight something…

How did [CHARACTER NAME] + [SHORT CHARACTER DESCRIPTION] end up [CONFLICT, OPPOSITE OF CHARACTER DESCRIPTION]

However, everything changes when…

Hunted by…

If [CONFLICT] isn't bad enough, now…

If they find out…

In a [SETTING] that runs on…here finally is a [CHARACTER] who cannot…[CONFLICT]

In the face of…

Initially seems like…but then…

It all starts with…

It doesn't help that…

It's all routine until…

It's bad enough that…

It's the last thing…

Just when she's fallen in love…

Kicked off

Knocked unconscious

Learns two things: [SET UP DRAMATIC TENSION WITH CONFLICTING DISCOVERIES]

Life is hell for...but especially bad for...

Love triangle

Making a pact with [ANTAGONISTS, VIOLENT GROUP OR OTHER BAD GUYS/GIRLS] may be the only way to...

Mix-up

Most people...[CHARACTER] + [EXACT OPPOSITE]

Must fight to…

Mystery surrounding…

Never once questioned...

No means of survival

No way out

Not a problem until…

Not an accident

Not the only one with secrets to hide

Now [CHARACTER] is faced with a dangerous choice

Now [CHARACTERS] are on the run

Now she's face to face with…

Now there's a [LIST OF STORY CONFLICTS OR COMPLICATIONS]

Now, [CHARACTER] has two choices: [CHOICE] or [CHOICE]

Nowhere to run

On the run and trapped by a…

One thing stands between [CHARACTER] and…

One thing stands between…

Only a few months into…

Only facing [CONFLICT, CRISES, FEAR] can save her.

Only to discover…

Only to find…

Only to learn…

Opportunity turns into a nightmare when…

Outside the law

Personal vendetta against…

Pits himself against…

Plagued by…

Promise

Proof she's threatening to use to…

Pursued by…

Pushed to the brink of...

Puts him on the radar of...

Questioning everything he thought he knew about...

Questioning everything she's known

Rebels against...

Rejected by...he's waging a personal war against...as a last resort.

Relationship reaches a breaking point

Rogue cops

Runs for his life

Set up a trap to...

Sets him in his sights

Sets off a chain of events

Setting in motion events that

Setting into motion...

Sever ties

Shattered by the knowledge that...

She can no longer...

She can't avoid...

She can't seem to stay away from...

She doesn't trust him

She finds companionship with [CHARACTER WITH CONFLICT].

She must confront...or...

She must endure...

She runs afoul of...

She tackles the...

She's being set up for the murder

She's desperate enough to...

Snowball effect...

So when [CHARACTER] is asked to...[CONFLICT], she is in.

Someone inside the [SETTING] is [CONFLICT], [CONFLICT] and [CONFLICT].

Someone is [CONFLICT] the [SPECIFC GROUP OR SUBGROUP] of [SETTING].

Something she has never had to face before...

Spirals out of control

Stop the [CONFLICT] that destroyed her family

Strange disappearance

Stumbles into...

Sucked into....

Suddenly...

Summoned back to...by...

Surrounded by deception

Suspects [CHARACTER] isn't the [ROLE, JOB, POSITION] she claims to be

Swept into...

Take him out

Takes a violent turn

Tangled up in…

That all changes when…

That changes when…

The [CHARACTERS] from [SETTING] only complicate things.

The answers she finds reveal…

The closer he gets to…the more…

The hunter becomes the hunted

The last thing he needs is…

The little matter of [BIG MATTER, CONFLICT, etc.]

The next morning, however…

The only thing more troubling than…is…

The only thing standing in her way…

The problem is…

The threat of [CONFLICT]

The unthinkable happens

Then a chance reunion with…

Then he learns that...

Then into the [SETTING] falls [CHARACTER], a [CHARACTER DESCRIPTION]

Then she meets…

There is something wrong with...

They [SHOCKING ACTION] and made it home in time for [MUNDANE ACTION]

They face opposition at every turn

They face opposition at every turn, first by...then by...

Things all go to hell

This revelation horrifies him

Threatens to...

Thrown into...

To get away with it, she'll need to [CONFLICT].

To make matters worse...

To reach his goal, he'll have to outmaneuver...

Too bad...

Torn between...

Toughest case

Triggering events...

Trouble is...

Turned sour

Turns the full weight of...against her

Turns up dead

Ultimate target

Uncover a conspiracy

Uncover evidence of...

Unfortunately, this all happens at the same time...

Unfortunately...

Unlikely adversary

Until a twist of fate...

Until he finds himself...

Until he rejects...

Until one day...

Until the unthinkable happens

Unwittingly thrust into...

Very thing he fears the most

Wage a battle against...

Waging a personal war against...

Waking up to find...

What [CHARACTER] doesn't know...

What starts as...turns into...

When [CHARACTER] is... she has no idea her life is about to change forever...

When [CHARACTER] shows up at...she stumbles into...

When [CHARACTER] turns out to be...

When [CHARACTERS] learn...

When [CONFLICT, CRISES, INCITING EVENT], [CHARACTER]...

When [CONFLICT], [CHARACTER] faces an insurmountable problem: [CONFLICT], [CONFLICT] and [CONFLICT].

When [CONFLICT], she must decide...

When he stumbles into...

When his [CHARACTER] shows up on his doorstep...

When she finally comes close…

When the truth of [CHARACTER]'s past is revealed…

When…[CHARACTER] must make a choice: [TWO OPPOSING CHOICES].

When…goes terribly wrong...

When…he decides to take a terrifying risk...

When…the last thing he expected was...

When…accidently…

While…[CHARACTER] finds a…

With a relentless [ANTAGONIST] trailing them…

With his knowledge of…[CHARACTER] renounces…and chooses…

Worst fears are realized…

Worst thing about…

Goal

[CHARACTER] + [CHARACTER DESCRIPTION] in [SETTING] hopes for [GOAL]. But…[CONFLICT]

[CHARACTER] and her friend [CHARACTER] journey through [SETTING]…to [GOAL] and [GOAL], although doing so may [STAKES]

[CHARACTER] dreams of…

[CHARACTER] has a chance to…

[CHARACTER] has a simple plan: [GOAL], [GOAL] and [GOAL].

[CHARACTER] has his life planned: [GOAL], [GOAL] and [GOAL].

[CHARACTER] has to…before…

[CHARACTER] has tried to [GOAL], tried to [GOAL] and [GOAL], even though she's [CONFLICT]

[CHARACTER] has two main desires in life: [INSERT PAIR OF HUMOROUS OR CONFLICTING GOALS].

[CHARACTER] is determined to prove…

[CHARACTER] is determined to…

[CHARACTER] knows she must [GOAL]

[CHARACTER] knows there must be a better way to [GOAL] – and he finds it in...

[CHARACTER] must [GOAL] to save…

[CHARACTER] must…or die trying.

[CHARACTER] races to…but discovers…

[CHARACTER] scrambles to [GOAL], while [ANTAGONIST or CONFLICT] closes in...

[CHARACTER] sees an opportunity to…

[CHARACTER] sees the [SETTING, OPPORTUNITY] as a chance to [GOAL]

[CHARACTER] sets out to discover…

[CHARACTER] sets out to find…

[CHARACTER] uses the [MAJOR ELEMENT OF THE STORY] to not only [EXTERNAL GOAL] but also to [INTERNAL GOAL], [EMOTIONAL, RELATIONAL GOAL] and [EMOTIONAL, RELATIONAL GOAL]

[CHARACTER] vows to solve the puzzle.

[CHARACTER] will do anything to [GOAL]

[CHARACTER] would love to be [GOAL] but [CONFLICT]

A [CHARACTER] who wants [GOAL].

After...their only goal is...

All [CHARACTER] can think about is...

All [CHARACTER] wants is...

All she wants is [GOAL]

All she's ever wanted

Armed with...[CHARACTER] retraces...

Begins a journey to…

But [ACHIEVING HIS/HER GOAL] could come at the cost of his/her [STAKES]

But [CHARACTER AGE] + [CHARACTER NAME] has a secret: she wants [GOAL].

But [CHARACTER]'s [GOAL] proves stronger than [OPPOSITVE GOAL]

But [GOAL] could be the worst thing

But [GOAL] isn't as easy as [ACTION]

Catch the killer

Clear her name

Dead-set on…

Desperate to find answers…

Determined to tell the truth

Determined to…

Devise a plan to [GOAL]

Driven by...

Enticed by the [GOAL]

Escape the memory

First, he must...

Fulfill her promise

He must find a way to...

He plans to [GOAL] but [CONFLICT].

He resolves to...

He wants to know if there is a connection between...

Hellbent on...

Her hopes of [GOAL] are few and far between...

Her only chance to [GOAL].

His duty is clear...

His most burning desire: [GOAL].

His objective is singular...

If [CHARACTER] can just [STEP TOWARD THE GOAL], she might be able to [ULTIMATE GOAL]

If [CHARACTER] could...he might be able to...

If she is to...she must...

Intent on...

Keep the promise

Launches a dangerous plan to...

Lured by [GOAL]

Makes it her mission to…

More than anything, the [CHARACTERS] want…

Needs to… before…

Newfound purpose

Now [CHARACTER] must...

Now [CHARACTER] will do anything to…

Now he must prove his innocence

Now she must…

One chance to [POSITIVE GOAL] and to prevent [NEGATIVE GOAL, CONFLICT]

Only by…can she…

Only want one thing…

Only wants to…

Prove herself

Puts her on the trail of…

Redeem herself

Save her…

Save the [GOAL] once and for all

Second chance at love

Seizing her chance to…

Sets her sights

Sets out to find answers

She believes it's finally her chance to...

She can finally [GOAL]

She has one mission: [GOAL]

She sets out to…

She'll do anything to uncover the truth…

Since...hasn't...the only way to [GOAL]

Solve a murder

Stop the curse

Stop the killer

Stop the wedding…

The hunt for…

The only obstacle to [GOAL] is [CONFLICT, OTHER COMPETING GOAL]

Their only chance to [GOAL] is to [GOAL, CONFLICT].

This is her chance to…

Throws himself into the...

Together they might be able to [GOAL] if they don't kill each other first.

Unfortunately, getting [GOAL] turns out to be the easy part.

Unless they can find a way to…

When [CHARACTER] discovers…he sets his sights on [GOAL]

Will do anything to...

With his last chance to [GOAL] slipping away...

Power Words

Abomination

Agony

Alias

Alliance

Ancient

Armed

Assassin

Attraction

Awkward

Awry

Backfires

Banished

Believing

Betrayed

Bizarre

Bombarded

Bone

Branded

Breakthrough

Brutal

Bullet

Cabal

Chained

Chaos

Chemistry

Chilling

Chosen

Clashes

Coax

Cocky

Collapse

Collapsed

Compelled

Confession

Confidential

Confront

Conniving

Contagious

Controlling

Convicted

Convinced

Cursed

Deadly

Debilitating

Decadent

Decimated

Deepened

Deeper

Desire

Diabolical

Disaster

Discord

Discovers

Disembark

Disillusioned

Displaced

Dissension

Distraught

Distressed

Divorced

Driven

Drown

Ekes

Elite

Embark

Enigmatic

Entangled

Evil

Except…

Exclusive

Exile

Facade

Fallout

Fantasies

Feud

Flee

Forbidding

Forced

Forensic

Forge

Forged

Forsake

Fragile

Fringe

Fringes

Fumbled

Grind

Grudge

Guilt

Gunman

Harvesting

Haunted

Heartbreak

Horrific

Hostile

Hunted

If…

Illegal

Imprisoned

Improvised

Incalculable

Infested

Infiltrated

Insidious

Instead…

Intense

Intrigue

Jeopardy

Kidnapped

Lethal

Liaison

Lies

Love

Lure

Lured

Magic

Marked

Menacing

Mesmerized

Monster

Mystical

Notorious

Obsessed

Obsession

Operative

Orchestrate

Outlast

Overworked

Pawn

Payback

Plague

Powerful

Predator

Prestigious

Pretends

Prevent

Provoke

Prowling

Puzzle

Rage

Raw

Reawakened

Redeem

Reemerge

Regret

Rekindled

Relationship

Relentless

Remnant

Renounce

Rescued

Resurface

Retaliation

Revenge

Rift

Ruthless

Sadistic

Scandalous

Scarred

Scheme

Scientific

Scorned

Scrambling

Secrets

Seduction

Shooter

Showdown

Simmering

Skewered

Sniper

Soon…

Steamy

Stranded

Stripped

Succumbed

Summon

Surrogate

Sworn

Symbols

Taken

Tame

Target

Tension

Transgression

Traumatic

Treason

Triggering

Troublesome

Troubling

True love

Twisted

Ultimately

Underworld

Undone

Unearth

Unexpectedly

Unexplained

Unimaginable

Unknown

Unleashing

Unless…

Unlock

Vanished

Warpath

While…

Years

Questions (Pitch)

How far would you go to…?

What could go wrong?

What could she know…?

What if you found a way to…?

What's [CHARACTER NAME] – a [TRAIT], [TRAIT] and [TRAIT] – to do?

What would happen if…?

Will he…? Or will he…?

Will it be too late?

Will she be able to…?

Setting

[CHARACTER] escapes to…

[CHARACTER] has never left...

[CHARACTER] retreats to

[CHARACTER] sets off for…

[CHARACTER] sets out to search for answers on the [SETTING]

[CITY]'s trendy [DISTRICT NAME] district

[DATE]: [CONFLICT]

[TITLE] takes them from [SETTING] to [SETTING]

A world where…

Abandoned village

Aboard the...

Ancient trade route

And... finally land them in [SETTING], and [CHARACTER] finally has a chance to...

Back in...

Banished to [SETTING]

Bohemian

But in a [SETTING] where nobody plays by the rules...

But trapped together in the [SETTING]...

Cover for...

Crumbling

Deep into the heart of...

Divided by...

Epic quest through...

Flees to...

Forced to return to [SETTING]

From the [SETTING TRAIT] of [SETTING], through the [SETTING TRAIT] of [SETTING] to the [SETTING TRAIT] of [SETTING]...

From...to...

Front for...

Future

Gritty world of...

He heads toward...

His homeland, [SETTING/NAME OF HOMELAND]

His journey takes her...

Hometown

Icelandic countryside

In [SETTING]...

In a [SETTING] in [LARGER SETTING]

In a country of...

In a dangerous world of...

In a setting where...

In a world filled with...

In a world where...

In an atmosphere thick with...

In present-day [CITY]...

In the fall of [YEAR]...

In the span of...

Intelligence agency

International

It has been seven years since...

It's the year...

It's... [YEAR OF STORY]

Labyrinth

Lost city

Mountain prison

Navigate the…

Oldest Victorian house…

Only in a place where…can he [GOAL] and [GOAL]

Plantation

Prestigious

Remote

Rubble strewn

Ruins

Seedy underbelly

Set against the emotionally charged backdrop of…

Set in a world inspired by…

Set in late Victorian England

Set in the fictional city of…

Set in the fictitious town of…

Set in the imaginary city of….

Set in the world of [WORLD OF YOUR STORY – i.e. engineers, 4-H steer competitions, etc.]

Since the [SETTING] was [CONFLICT]…

Stranded

The last place he wants to be is…

The novel begins in…

The year is [YEAR]. The place is [SETTING].

Through the worlds of…

Thrown reluctantly into the world of...

Tiny

Top-secret

Toxic

Transports readers to [SETTING], [SETTING] and [SETTING]

Travels from [SETTING] to [SETTING]

Tropical

Turn of the 20th Century

Unlike any place she's ever known

Urban

When [CHARACTER] returns to [SETTING]

Wilderness

World's biggest

Stakes

[CHARACTER] keeps [SECRET] a secret from [OTHER CHARACTER] fearing that [STAKES]

[CHARACTER'S LIFE, SALVATION, HUMAN EXISTENCE] depends upon [CHARACTER] + [GOAL, ACTION, COMPLETING TASK]

Afraid of ending up in...

Afraid of...

Almost certain death

At any cost

Before she is...forever

But with [STAKES OR CONFLICT], he'll do anything to [GOAL].

Decide once and for all

Despite the risk

Even at the cost of…

Even if it means…

Even if that means…

Everything to lose

Give up everything

Global catastrophe

Grave danger

Hangs in the balance

He races to [GOAL] before they force him to make an impossible choice: [CHOICE #1 with STAKES] or [CHOICE #2 with STAKES].

He risks losing it all

His only hope is…

If [CHARACTER] can't somehow...then...

If [CHARACTER] doesn't...[GOAL] in [TIME FRAME] ...[STORY STAKES].

If he fails to...then...

If he fights, he risks losing [STAKES] and destroying [STAKES].

If he runs… [STAKES]. If he fights… [STAKES].

If he wants…he has to give up…

If she continues to…then…

If she fails…

If she is to walk away unscathed…

If they don't…

Lead to his death

Lose everything he holds dear

Loses the one thing she loves most

Lost his chance at…

Meet his deadline

No one is safe

Not only [PERSON, GROUP, PLACE], but [OTHER PERSON, GROUP, PLACE OR CONCEPT], may be at stake.

Only a great sacrifice will allow them to...

Or die trying

Or risk losing everyone he holds dear

Otherwise…

Price of…

Put his own life on the line

Risked everything

Risks his life

She'll have to risk [STAKES] and accept the aid of [CHARACTER] + [CHARACTER DESCRIPTION] to survive.

Should they fail...

Steep cost

That might kill him before he can decide

The one chance to love

The one secret [CHARACTER] must keep, or risk...

The one thing she can't exist without

Threatens to destroy everything

To avoid [STAKES], [CHARACTER]...

Ultimate sacrifice

Unthinkable cost

With lives on the line…

Ticking Clock

[CHARACTER] only has [TIME FRAME] left...

[NUMBER] months to live

All before…

And she'd better hurry, or…

As the [ANTAGONIST] closes in…

As the clock ticks away…

Before…

Before another girl goes missing

Before he marries the wrong woman

Before his time runs out...

Before it's too late

Before the killer strikes again

Before the spell wears off

Before times runs out

Before…

But will she be fast enough?

Every [TIMEFRAME]…

Find the killer before…

Frantically tries to...

Getting closer and closer

If [CHARACTER] doesn't...[GOAL] in [TIME FRAME]...[STORY STAKES].

If it's not too late

If she can't...before…

It is three days before…

It won't be long before…

Last chance to…

Little time to...

May be closer than he thinks

No time to rest

Now she has one hour to...

On the brink of…

One wrong move...

Only one shot to…

Quickly

Race to escape

Real fast

She must… before…

Solve the case fast

Soon they are racing…

Stop… before…

The clock is ticking

Time is running out

Twisting tighter and tighter…

Under intense pressure

Urgent

While [ANTAGONIST OR ANOTHER OBSTACLE] closes in…

With time running out…

Transition Words

After

As

Before

Except

Instead

Now

Soon

Then

Unless

Until

When

While

SECTION 3:
BOOK DETAILS SWIPE FILE

In the Book Details section of a query letter, you highlight anything unique or special about your book, and, if you haven't already done so earlier in your letter, you share the book genre, word-count, mention that it's complete and part of a series (if applicable) and possibly compare your book to other popular books in your genre.

Let's turn that into a bulleted list so that it's easy for you to apply to your own query letter:

- Anything unique or special about your book
- Book genre
- Word-count
- Mention that the book is completed
- Mention that the book is part of a series or has series potential
- Compare your book to other popular books in your genre

As mentioned earlier, you can choose to include the book details at the beginning or near the end of a query letter. I've seen it done either way in effective query letters so there is no single right way.

The important thing is to concisely and creatively share the title, genre, word count and uniqueness of your novel.

In other words, there are many ways to handle this section. In this swipe file, you will find some of the most effective tricks and tactics published authors use to leverage the power of BOOK DETAILS.

Note: For clarity, I want to point out that the very first template is an actual parenthetical phrase that would be put inside parenthesis in the actual query letter. It can be copied and pasted directly into your query, if you wish.

Book Details Swipe File

(Please see attached sample chapters)

[FAMOUS EDITOR, BESTSELLING AUTHOR OR WELL-KNOWN PUBLISHING FIGURE] is currently reading my manuscript

[FILM COMPANY] (Producer of [MOVIE] and [OTHER MOVIE]) has expressed interest in optioning the film rights

[GENRE] at [WORD COUNT] words with an [BESTSELLING NOVEL IN YOUR GENRE] feel

[GENRE] that reinvents [MYTH, FAIRY TALE, ETC] from the perspective of...

[POPULAR BOOK IN YOUR GENRE] meets [ANOTHER POPULAR BOOK]

[TITLE] + [WORD COUNT] is a finalist in the [NAME OF SPECIFIC CONTEST] contest

[TITLE] (80,000 words) is a [GENRE] novel with a [GENRE, POPULAR NOVEL OR MOVIE OR TV SERIES] twist

[TITLE] begins as a [GENRE] reminiscent of [BESTSELLING NOVEL] but then spirals into a [ANOTHER GENRE]

[TITLE] combines the [DESCRIBE WRITING STYLE] of [BESTSELLING AUTHOR] with the [DESCRIBE DIFFERENT WRITING STYLE] of [ANOTHER BESTSELLING AUTHOR IN YOUR GENRE]

[TITLE] has been well received on...

[TITLE] includes...

[TITLE] is a [GENRE] with an [OTHER GENRE OR SUBGENRE] slant, complete at [WORD COUNT].

[TITLE] is a [GENRE] with series potential

[TITLE] is a [WORD COUNT] + [GENRE] aptly described as [BESTSELLER IN YOUR GENRE] meets [BESTSELLER IN YOUR GENRE]

[TITLE] is a [WORD COUNT] + [GENRE] with a twist

[TITLE] is a blend of [FAMOUS BOOK OR MOVIE] and [BESTSELLER]

[TITLE] is a story of...

[TITLE] is complete at 110,000 words

[TITLE] is complete at just over...

[TITLE] is my [WORD COUNT]-word chapter book written for a [GRADE] reading level

[TITLE] is the first in a planned series

[TITLE] is the story of a struggle between…

[TITLE] treads the line between…

[TITLE] works as either a standalone or the beginning of a series.

[TITLE], a [WORD COUNT] + [GENRE], is complete

[TITLE], complete at [WORD COUNT] words, aims to appeal to readers who enjoyed the [STORY ELEMENT] in [BESTSELLING BOOK TITLE] and the [STORY ELEMENT] in [BESTELLER BOOK TITLE.]

A [WORD COUNT] reimagining of the [IDENTIFY LEGEND] legend

A cross between…

A retelling of…

Aims to appeal to those who enjoyed…

Amateur sleuth

Based on a true story

Blend of mystery and suspense…

Blended with equal parts [GENRE, TONE] and [GENRE, TONE]

Character-driven [STORY ELEMENT] of [BESTSELLING NOVEL] written with the mainstream undercurrents of [BESTSELLING AUTHOR].

Complete manuscript at just over [WORD COUNT] words,

Contemporary romance

Cozy Mystery

Crime Thriller

Crossover novel

Draws on aspects of my past…

Dual narrative

Dusted with…

Dystopian

Edgy thriller

Emotional depth

Emotionally resonate thriller

Equal parts [GENRE] and [GENRE]

Erotica

Explores the power of...

Fans of the TV mini-series [TV SERIES OF SAME OR SIMILAR GENRE] will love the…

Fans of...will enjoy similar elements and a strong [CHARACTER TYPE] voice.

Fantasy

First in a trilogy

Fit on the bookshelf between…

Fit your tastes

Given the public's recent fascination with…

High Fantasy

Historical

Humorous

Humorous, rhyming picture book

I am currently outlining the sequel

I believe [TITLE] will make a good addition to your list.

I believe the market is ripe for a story like mine.

I have just begun another book set in the same world.

I like to think of it as [TITLE OF BESTSELLING BOOK IN YOUR GENRE] meets [OTHER TITLE OF BESTSELLING BOOK IN YOUR GENRE].

I might pitch it as…

I refer to my book as….

I'm currently working on the next in the series…

If [BESTSELLING AUTHOR] and [OTHER BESTSELLING AUTHOR] wrote a book together, [TITLE] might be the result.

In a setting that evokes [REAL SETTING LOCATION] and [REAL SETTING LOCATION].

In style, it will resonate with readers of [BOOK TITLE OF BESTSELLER IN YOUR GENRE]

In terms of content and theme, [BESTSELLER BOOK TITLE IN SAME GENRE] recounts a similar story of...

In the vein of...

Inspirational

Inspired by...

Interwoven stories

It combines the [ELEMENTS OF A BESTSELLER] of [BESTSELLER BOOK TITLE] with the [ELEMENTS OF ANOTHER BESTSELLER] of [BESTSELLER BOOK TITLE]

It finds its roots in...

It has the [DESCRIBE MOOD] mood of [TITLE OF BESTSELLING BOOK IN YOUR GENRE], along with the politics of [ANOTHER BESTSELLING BOOK IN YOUR GENRE].

It is similar to...

It is the tale of how...

It is told in alternating point-of-view chapters from...

It twists conventional [TYPE OF STORIES] stories into...

It will appeal to readers of [TITLE OF POPULAR BOOK IN SAME GENRE]

It's a [GENRE] with a [NUMBER] word count.

It's about time someone told the truth about…

It's a story of…

It's told in tandem between...

It's… meets… steeped in…

Mainstream

Middle Grade

Might appeal to readers whose tastes fall between [BESTSELLING AUTHOR IN SAME GENRE] and [ANOTHER BESTSELLING AUTHOR IN SAME GENRE]

Modern-day retelling of...

Multiple POV

Mystery

New Adult

Noir

[BESTSELLING AUTHOR]'s + [RELEVANT BOOK TITLE FROM THAT AUTHOR]

Please note that I am querying other agents…

Police Procedural

Populated with characters reminiscent of…

Potential for a series set in the same world

Professionally edited manuscript

Provides glimpses into [PEOPLE GROUP, STORY WORLD, PROFESSION] life

Psychological suspense

Quirky characters of....

Racially diverse

Regency Romance

Science Fiction

Sets up plot threads for at least one sequel.

Standalone [GENRE] novel complete at [WORD COUNT]

Steampunk

Steamy heat

Story elements

Strong central love story

Strong potential to cross into the adult market

Suitable for…

Suspense

Sweet Romance

That could be described as....

That will appeal to...

The first in a planned [NUMBER] book series

The novel is aimed at the [MARKET NAME] market, and deals with [NAME ISSUES] issues faced by [SPECIFIC READER DEMOGRAPHIC].

This book has a unique point of view

This book is based on…

This book is unique because...

This is a multiple submission…

This is a story of…

This novel was inspired by…

Thriller

Thriller with speculative elements

Told from alternating points of view…

Told from the perspectives of…

Told in [NUMBER] POVs…

Told through [CHARACTER]'s letters to…

Told through [CHARACTER]'s past and present narrative…

Touches on…

Transports readers to [SETTING], [SETTING] and [SETTING]

Upmarket women's fiction

Weaves back and forth between the present and [YEAR or TIME PERIOD].

With [GENRE] elements

With a splash of …

Woven together with…

Young Adult

Special Circumstance: Bestseller Book Series Template

What if you want to move beyond simply stating your book has "series potential" to more fully flesh out your series ideas? Here's a nice trilogy template to copy in the Book Details section of your query:

[TITLE] is the first in a thrilling trilogy about… which fans of…will enjoy. In the second novel, [TITLE OF SECOND

BOOK], [CHARACTER] + [CONFLICT, INCITING EVENT]. She/he embarks on a journey to [GOAL], and in the process [MORE CONFLICT or SHOCKING REVELATION], a twist that leads to the third novel, [TITLE OF THIRD BOOK].

SECTION 4:
BIO SWIPE FILE (OPTIONAL)

The author bio is <u>optional</u>. I repeat: it's totally, 100% optional.

In fact, it's the ONLY optional part of a query letter. Think about that.

I'm emphasizing this point because the **most common error in the bio is including one**. Most new authors don't have anything worth including in a bio and are much better off skipping it entirely. This is normal, predictable and agents "get" it.

What *IS* the bio? A bio is a list of credentials that build credibility and demonstrate platform. A bio is what makes you look good to the agent. Remember, a query is a sales letter. You want to put in what sells the book and leave out what distracts an agent from requesting your manuscript and offering representation.

For fiction, the bio is only relevant if you have won <u>major national awards</u>, if you know <u>famous authors</u> (your father is Dean Koontz), if you have a <u>significant </u>personal experience that relates to the topic of your novels (you were kidnapped by pirates and held hostage for 10 years) or if you have built a <u>national platform</u> from which to sell your books.

The bio is a sales tool. If you think your bio ups your chance of representation, include it. Otherwise, skip it. A bad bio is worse than no bio.

So, if that is true, then why even include a Bio Swipe File in this book then? Because I wanted to create a book that grows with you, that is just as helpful to you as a writer with no experience as it is when you have reams of publications and awards behind you.

Bio Swipe File

A short story of mine recently won first place in the [PRESTIGIOUS CONTEST NAME].

As you may remember…

Bestselling Author, [AUTHOR NAME], mentored me for 3 years.

Bestselling Author, [AUTHOR NAME], said of my novel: "[AWESOME QUOTE]".

I am a [SUBJECT] teacher who has traveled to [SETTING OF NOVEL] for research

I am a graduate of [FAMOUS, RESPECTED CREATIVE WRITING SCHOOL]

I am a member of…

I am an Associate Editor at…

I am currently published through [MAJOR PUBLISING COMPANY].

I am the recipient of [NATIONAL AWARD or WELL-RESPECTED AWARD].

I enjoy being an active member of…

I have a Masters in English from [PRESTIGIOUS SCHOOL]

I have already received blurbs for the manuscript from such notable figures as [NAMES OF BESTSELLING AUTHORS, EXPERTS, etc.]

I have been accepted on the…

I have been writing professionally for [NUMBER OF] years

I have ghostwritten for…

I have previously published…

I have won the [NATIONAL AWARD]

I have written several…that have received national attention

I hold an MFA in Creative Writing from…

I serve as President of the [LOCAL CHAPTER OF NATIONAL WRITING ORGANIZATION].

I was kidnapped and held hostage for 15 years by terrorists

I was named a finalist in…

I write [GENRE] and [GENRE].

I wrote this manuscript while finishing my MFA in…at…

I'm a freelance writer whose work has appeared in…

I'm an active member of the [NAME OF SPECIFIC CHAPTER] chapter of the [WRITER'S NATIONAL ORGANIZATION SUCH AS MWA OR RWA]

My [GENRE], [TITLE], will be released by [NAME OF PUBLISHER] in [SEASON] [YEAR].

My debut novel, [TITLE] was released through [NAME OF PUBLISHER, PRESS] in [MONTH] [YEAR]

My experience with…

My fiction has appeared in…

My novel took first place in [NATIONAL FICTION CONTEST]

My previous manuscript, a [GENRE], achieved [NUMBER] contest placements.

My screenplays have been shortlisted for several major awards

My short story, [TITLE] was recently nominated for a [PRESTEGIOUS PRIZE or AWARD].

My stories have appeared in…

My stories have been published in…

My website is [WEBSITE]

My work has appeared in…

My writing credentials include…

New York Times Bestselling Author [NAME OF BESTSELLING AUTHOR] recently endorsed my novel [TITLE]: [ENDORSEMENT].

Quotes from my [BOOK, NOVEL, STORY, ARTICLE, etc.] were used in…

This manuscript was awarded…

Why am I the one to write this book?

SECTION 5:
SALUTATION SWIPE FILE

The end of a query letter is intended to be a short and sweet goodbye, heralded by appreciation and brief mention of any included materials (synopsis, sample chapters, etc.). As you will see, there are plenty of variations on *how* to say what's included, thank you and goodbye, but the main point is to say it quickly and be done.

You may notice the slight variation of phrases such as "I have enclosed" and "I have pasted below". I included these differences to show how to query both through postal mail and through email. Some agencies even require authors to fill out an online "query" submission form. The more options you have at your disposal, the better your chances of not getting stuck so you can move on to attracting an agent.

For those new to querying, a simultaneous submission is when you send your query to more than one agent at a time. This is a very common practice that most publishing experts (even literary agents) promote.

A few additional suggestions may be useful here:

- Keep the Salutation section brief
- Follow the submission guidelines of the agent (each agent is different and you can usually find this information on their agent website)
- Don't beg, don't make promises and (please, for the sake of all things literary) don't make threats

Also, don't underestimate this (or any) part of a query letter. You never know what word, phrase or statement might push the agent over the edge to request a partial or full manuscript. Small words can make big impacts.

Salutation Swipe File

A synopsis and the first 10 pages are pasted below, per your guidelines.

Best regards

Best wishes

I am grateful for your time and consideration.

I am happy to forward any materials (including the full manuscript) upon request.

I am prepared to send the complete manuscript upon request.

I have attached a one-page synopsis

I have enclosed...

I have included [INSERT INCLUDED PAGES, SYNOPSIS, etc.], just to give you a taste.

I have included...

I have pasted a writing sample below.

I have pasted below...

I hope that you will be interested in my...

I hope you consider representing my work

I look forward to hearing from you

I may be contacted by email at [EMAIL] or by cell phone at [PHONE]

I would love to hear from you, [AGENT NAME], if [TITLE] is a manuscript you would like to further explore.

I would love to send you...

I'd be delighted to send a sample chapter or the full manuscript at your request

I'd be happy to supply the full manuscript.

If you would like a larger sample, or the entire manuscript, you may contact me using the information below my signature

I'm including the first few pages of [TITLE] below to give you an idea of the tone of the writing.

May I send you the completed manuscript?

My first 50 pages are enclosed

My first five pages

Per the guidelines on your website...

Per your submission guidelines...

Please let me know if you would like sample chapters

Please let me know if you would like to read [TITLE].

Please note that this is a simultaneous submission

Respectfully

Sincerely

Thank you for reading.

Thank you for your time and consideration

Thank you once again for your time and your consideration of my work. I look forward to hearing from you.

The first five pages are included at the end of this email for your consideration.

The first 10 pages are pasted below.

The full manuscript is available upon request.

The manuscript is available, in part of full, upon request

The synopsis and fist five pages follow my signature block

This is an exclusive that expires on [DATE].

Upon your request, I would be happy to provide the complete manuscript.

SECTION 6:
QUERY TEMPLATES

By now, you have a massive list of exact words, phrases and sentence templates to shift an agent from "I don't know" to "I have to read this!"

I don't know about you but I'm overwhelmed with excitement about sharing this resource with other writers. This one book really can help you write the letter that changes your life forever.

But there is still more I want to share with you. Singular words, phrases and even entire sentence templates are helpful, but the real magic comes when you start to combine these templates into fully formed paragraphs.

For example, to hook an agent right from the beginning, you might combine templates to create something like this:

> As a regular reader of your blog, I noticed that you recently stated that you were looking for [INSERT DIRECT QUOTE FROM AGENT]. Therefore, I'd like to offer my [WORD COUNT] + [GENRE] novel, [TITLE] for your consideration.

Ok, *that's* a template. How might it look fully fleshed out with details? Here's an example: (Note: I left in the brackets to highlight the inserted information. The brackets would be removed prior to actual submission).

> As a regular reader of your blog, I noticed that you recently stated that you were looking for ["Edgy thrillers with a strong female lead"]. Therefore, I'd like to offer my [83,000-word] + [Thriller] novel, [SISTER'S CURSE] for your consideration.

See how that works? You can mix and match the words,

phrases and templates in this book to generate an almost unlimited variation of query letter. That gives you more options, which dramatically boosts your odds of garnering agent attention, requests and representation.

Important Reminder: The words, phrases and templates in this book are meant to be springboards for your own creativity. You don't have to use any of the specific ideas presented here – you can create your own! The examples in this book have worked but they are not the only ideas that work. Feel free to use them, not use them or combine and experiment with them.

Merged Templates for Hooks, Pitches, Book Details, Bios and Salutations

Let's look at a few examples of full templates for hooks, pitches, book details, bios and salutations. Don't worry if, initially, you feel confused over what exactly to insert into the brackets. I've tried to make it as simple as possible, but reading the brackets can be tricky until you get the hang of it.

Oh, and right after these examples, I've included a series of full query templates followed by a completed query (with information inserted into the brackets) using Template #1. By comparing the full template with the fleshed-out version of the compete query, you'll develop insight into how to best use the swipe files to write your own letter.

I want you to get a Ph.D. in query writing, so here we go…

Hooks

I'm submitting this completed [WORD COUNT] manuscript to you because of your interest in [GENRE].

I've read your [ARTICLES, BLOGS, INTERVIEWS, REVIEWS], and really connected with [PERSONAL

CONNECTION, THEME, ADVICE, etc.)! I'd be delighted if you'd consider my manuscript, [TITLE], for your list.

Thank you so much for agreeing to take a look at my manuscript, *[TITLE]*. I was excited to learn that you have worked with authors like [AUTHOR THE AGENT REPRESENTS] and [ANOTHER AUTHOR THE AGENT REPRESENTS] at [LITERARY AGENCY or PUBLISHING COMPANY]! I recently read [AUTHOR THE AGENT REPRESENTS]'s [TITLE OF BOOK FROM THE AUTHOR] and loved his/her portrayal of the [DESCRIBE CHARCTER], [CHARACTER NAME], not unlike [YOUR PROTAGONIST] in my book.

Pitches

[CHARACTER NAME]'s perfect [WORLD OF STORY or SETTING] life is transformed when she suddenly [CONFLICT] after his [CHARACTER] is [CONFLICT]. Instant [CONFLICT], after years of unsuccessful attempts to [GOAL], is both an exhilarating and terrifying prospect. [PROTAGONIST] struggles to [GOAL] as well as [ANOTHER GOAL]. [CHARACTER] is resistant to [WORLD OF THE STORY, SETTING or GOAL] and constantly [CONFLICT or PROBLEM]. The strain between [CHARACTER] and [CHARACTER] mounts as [CONFLICT] escalates. Instead of the [GOAL], [CHARACTER] feels as if her world is being torn apart by [CONFLICT], leaving her to question [WORLD OF STORY], [RELATIONSHIP, SUCH AS FATHERHOOD, MARRIAGE, ROLE AS CIA HANDLER, etc.], and [INTERNAL CONFLICT OVER GOAL].

When [CHARACTER] overhears [ANTAGONIST] plotting to [GOAL], he embarks on an adventure through [SETTING] to try to prevent [CONFLICT]. To succeed, he'll need to [CONFLICT], [CONFLICT], [CONFLICT] and [CONFLICT]. If he fails, not only will [STAKES], but [OTHER STAKES or ULTIMATE STAKES]. Together with [CHARACTER], he must defeat [ANTAGONIST] and reclaim [GOAL] before [CONFLICT] or else [STAKES].

Book Details

[TITLE] is a [GENRE] complete at [WORD COUNT]

I am seeking representation for [TITLE], a [WORD COUNT] + [GENRE].

Bios (Note: A bio is optional. If you don't have excellent, relevant credentials, skip it)

I'm the author of several novels published with [BIG PUBLISHING COMPANY] and have received [NATIONAL AWARDS or RECOGNITIONS]. I also have an MFA in [FOCUS OF MFA, such as CREATIVE WRITING] and my non-fiction writing has appeared in [NATIONAL PUBLICATION], [NATIONAL PUBLICATION], and other publications. I'm a [WRITING JOB or ROLE] for [NATIONAL PUBLICATION or PUBLISHING COMPANY].

My novel took first place in [NATIONAL FICTION CONTEST]. My work has also appeared in [NATIONAL PUBLICATIONS]. While writing this manuscript, I finished up my MFA at [SCHOOL NAME].

Salutations

I appreciate your time and interest in considering my query and I look forward to your response.

Per your submission guidelines, I've pasted the first ten pages below. The remainder is available at your request.

Thank you for your time and consideration.

Quick Start Guide – A Refresher

As a refresher, here is the Quick Start Guide again so that you can quickly and effortlessly craft your query letter from the swipe files. I've expanded the Second Fastest Method below now that you have read the majority of this book. It wouldn't have made sense earlier. You might want to keep this guide handy as you explore the full query templates.

Fastest Method

1. Read this entire book all the way through at least once
2. Choose one of the fully organized and written proven query templates (coming up very soon in this book!)
3. Insert your book details
4. Submit to agents & publishers!

Second Fastest Method

1. Read this entire book all the way through at least once
2. Choose words, phrases and sentence templates from each section (Hook, Pitch, Book Details, Bio, Salutation) that most relate to your book or story
   - Choose 1-3 Hook/Intro templates
   - Choose 5-7 Conflict templates
   - Choose 3-5 Compelling Phrases
   - Choose 5-7 Power Words
   - Choose 3-5 Transition Words
   - Choose 3-5 Character templates
   - Choose 1-3 Setting templates
   - Choose 2-3 Stakes templates
   - Choose 1-2 Ticking Clock templates
   - (OPTIONAL) Choose 1-3 Questions (Pitch)
   - (OPTIONAL) Choose 1-2 Bio templates (seriously consider skipping this step altogether – no really, skip it!)
   - Choose 1-3 Book Details
   - Choose 1-3 Salutation templates
3. Organize your words, phrases and sentences into a query structure (Hook, Pitch, Book Details, Bio, Salutation)

4. Insert your book details into the query, as needed
5. Submit to agents & publishers!

Full Copy-And-Paste Query Letter Templates

Now let's take it a step further.

Maybe you are still somewhat uncertain of how to proceed. Maybe you love the content in this book but you're not 100% sure how to translate the swipe files to the page or screen.

Don't worry. I have your back.

It's finally time to look at a set of complete query templates using a selected mash-up of swipe files ripped from this book. These are not the only templates – you can literally design hundreds or thousands of template variations from the swipe files.

You might be interested to know that I was able to create each template in less than 20 minutes. And it took me less than 60 minutes to transform Template #1 into a fully developed query that I'd submit with pride. You can read the complete query following the templates.

By the way, these templates are based on actual query letters that led to agent representation. The first template is based on a query that pulled in a mind-boggling 18 full manuscript requests and 5 offers of representation.

Now, those are query numbers to aim for!

Full Query Template #1

Dear [AGENT NAME],

I noticed on your Publisher's Marketplace page that you represent quite a few [GENRE] novels. Therefore, I'd like to offer my [WORD COUNT] + [GENRE] + [TITLE] for your consideration.

[AGE] + [CHARACTER] thinks [SETTING] would be perfect if he could just [GOAL]. [CONFLICT]. [CONFLICT]. And would it be too much to ask for [GOAL]. But when [CRISES/INCITING EVENT], he is [POWER WORD] into a new level of [SETTING] hell.

Now his [CHARACTER] + [CONFLICT], [ANOTHER CHARACTER] + [CONFLICT] and a group of [CHARACTERS] threaten to [CONFLICT] unless he [GOAL]. Soon he's sneaking into [SETTING], [ACTION] + [GOAL] and [ACTION] + [ANTAGONIST].

To make matters worse, he's finally [CONFLICT] + [CHARACTER] – only she might not [GOAL] when she finds out [REVELATION/SECRET]. [CHARACTER] needs to [GOAL] and [ANOTHER GOAL]. Otherwise, he can say goodbye to [STAKES/CONSEQUENCES], [STAKES] and any chance of [GOAL].

Per your submission guidelines, I have included [FOLLOW SUBMISSION GUIDELINES]. The full manuscript is available upon request. Thank you for your time and consideration.

Sincerely,

[AUTHOR NAME]

[AUTHOR CONTACT INFORMATION]

Full Query Template #2

Dear [AGENT NAME],

[MAIN CHARACTER] is running out of time. Her [CHARACTER] is [CONFLICT], the [CHARCTERS] want her [CONFLICT] and she's certain [CHARACTER] may [CONFLICT] at any moment. With no one left to trust, [CHARACTER] + [STAKES].

Then [CHARACTER] + [CHARACTER DESCRIPTION] arrives in [SETTING] saddled with [CONFLICT]. In a [SETTING] that runs on [SETTING DESCRIPTION], she [CONFLICT WITH SETTING DESCRIPTION]. [MAIN CHARACTER] has found someone she can [GOAL], but can [CHARACTER] + [GOAL] + [MAIN CHARACTER]. She finds herself in a dangerous game of [DESCRIBE GAME/CONFLICT] and she will be forced to choose between [GOAL] and [GOAL].

A tale of [GENRE CONVENTION], [GENRE CONVENTION] and [GENRE CONVENTION], [TITLE] should appeal to readers of [BESTSELLING AUTHOR]'s [BESTSELLER BOOK TITLE]. [YOUR BOOK TITLE] is complete at [WORD COUNT].

As per your agency's guidelines, I am including a [FOLLOW GUIDELINES – SYNOPSIS, SAMPLE CHAPTERS, etc.] and [FOLLOW GUIDELINES] as attachments. Thank you for your time.

Sincerely,

[AUTHOR NAME]

[AUTHOR CONTACT INFORMATION]

Full Query Template #3

Dear [AGENT NAME],

I am seeking representation for my [GENRE] novel, [TITLE], which is complete at [WORD COUNT] and has series potential.

A [CHARACTER TRAIT] + [CHARACTER TRAIT] + [CHARACTER ROLE] breaks into [SETTING] to [GOAL] before [STAKES] forever. To [GOAL], the [CHARACTER] must do the one thing he promised never to do – [ACTION OR TASK HE/SHE PROMISED NEVER TO DO].

Not only has [CHARACTER] spent the last decade [REASON HE/SHE CAN'T PERFORM ACTION OR TASK], he is also a [ROLE/STATUS THAT GIVES MORE REASON OR PRESSURE TO NOT PERFORM NEEDED ACTION OR TASK]. Making matters worse, his [OTHER CHARACTER] and [CHARACTER TRAIT/ROLE] will stop at nothing to [OPPOSING GOAL/CONFLICT], no matter the consequences.

[TITLE] will appeal to readers of [TITLE OF BESTSELLING BOOK IN YOUR GENRE] and [ANOTHER TITLE OF A BESTSELLING BOOK IN YOUR GENRE].

Thank you for your time and consideration.

Sincerely,

[AUTHOR NAME]

[AUTHOR CONTACT INFORMATION]

Full Query Template #4

Dear [AGENT],

[CHARACTER] knows how to [ACTION/TASK/CAREER], and she's especially great at [ANOTHER ACTION/TASK]. But when [CONFLICT] + [NUMBER] of [DAYS, WEEKS, MONTHS] before the [EVENT], [CHARACTER]'s world falls apart. She moves to [SETTING] and starts over. Thanks to her [TALENT, TRAIT, SKILL] and [OTHER TALENT, TRAIT, SKILLS], she [GOAL, GOOD FORTUNE, SUCCESS], until [CONFLICT] + [STAKES].

[CHARACTER] is not looking for [GOAL] – she's way too busy – and now she has a [GOAL], but she's having trouble ignoring the [CHARACTER DESCRIPTION] + [CHARACTER] and [ANOTHER CHARACTER] who [ACTION] + [DESCRIPTION OF ACTION]. She's so caught up in [GOAL/CONFLICT] that she doesn't notice that the [CHARACTER] who [ACTION/CONFLICT] has just [ACTION] – and has his sights set on [MAIN CHARACTER].

In [BESTSELLING AUTHOR IN YOUR GENRE] meets [BESTSELLING BOOK OR MOVIE IN YOUR GENRE], this story blends [GENRE COMPONENT], [GENRE COMPONENT] and [GENRE COMPONENT] with [GENRE COMPONENT]. [TITLE] is a [GENRE] novel complete at [WORD COUNT] with series potential.

Please note that this is a simultaneous submission. Thank you for your time and consideration.

Sincerely,

[AUTHOR NAME]

[AUTHOR CONTACT INFORMATION]

Full Query Template #5

Dear [AGENT],

[TITLE] is [GENRE] with [SPECIFIC STORY ELEMENTS] elements complete at [WORD COUNT] words.

Shortly after [AGE]-year-old [CHARACTER] discovers [DISCOVERY, CONFLICT], her [OTHER CHARACTER] + [CONFLICT] and [CONFLICT]. Abandoned by [CHARACTER, ROLE, PERSON], and with no knowledge of [HISTORY, SELF, ROLE, TALENT, POWER], [PROTAGONIST] wonders [SPECIFIC QUESTION ABOUT SELF]. All she wants is [GOAL] as far from [SETTING] as she can possibly get. Only in a place where [DETAILS OF SETTING] can she [GOAL] + [GOAL].

[OTHER MAIN CHARACTER, LOVE INTEREST] barely survived the [CONFLICT] that [CONSEQUENCE] and [CONSEQUENCE]. [ECHOES OR DETAILS OF THE CONFLICT] haunt his [IMPORTANT PART OF HIS LIFE], while [OTHER CONSQUENCES, ECHOES OR DETAILS OF CONFLICT] ruin his [ANOTHER IMPORTANT PART OF HIS LIFE]. He's lost all [SPECIFIC LOSS] and can't remember why he [PREVIOUS LIFE, PAST CAREER OR PASSION]. While [ACTION/TASK], [OTHER MAIN CHARACTER] finds [UNEXPECTED OBJECT] and [UNEXPECTED OBJECT]. Now he has a new mission: [GOAL]. A [GOAL] would go a long way toward [ULTIMATE GOAL]. Once he meets [PROTAGONIST], he doesn't want to jeopardize his chance to [GOAL].

[PROTAGONIST] and [OTHER MAIN CHARACTER] are drawn to each other, and a fragile [TYPE OF RELATIONSHIP – ALLIANCE, BOND, LOVE, FRIENDSHIP, etc.] begins to form—until [CONFLICT] and [CONFLICT]. She wants [GOAL]. Determined to [OPPOSITE GOAL OF PROTAGONIST], [OTHER MAIN CHARACTER] + [ACTION]. Then catastrophe strikes, setting off a chain of events that [CONFLICT/STAKES]. [PROTAGONIST] and [OTHER MAIN

CHARACTER] truly want to [MUTUAL GOAL], but with [CONFLICT], can they [GOAL]?

[TITLE] is the first book in a planned series. I have pasted [FOLLOW SUBMISSION GUIDELINE – SYNOPSIS, SAMPLE CHAPTERS, etc.] below my signature.

Sincerely,

[AUTHOR NAME]

[AUTHOR CONTACT INFORMATION

Christopher Kokoski

Complete Query Letter from Template #1

Shew! That's a lot to digest. Your mind may be spinning and it wouldn't surprise me if you aren't quite sure yet how to turn one of these templates into a full-fledged query letter.

Stay with me. I believe this section will help drive home exactly how to do just that.

As promised, here's a complete query letter fashioned from Template #1 with information inserted into the brackets. I've removed the brackets below to give the letter a better reading flow. I strongly encourage you to compare this complete query to the template to really absorb how to do this with your own story.

Dear Judith Marlin,

I noticed on your Publisher's Marketplace page that you represent quite a few Paranormal Young Adult novels. Therefore, I'd like to offer my 80,000-word Paranormal Young Adult novel, DEAD SPEAK, for your consideration.

14-year-old Bradley Ross thinks high school would be perfect if he could just stop dead people from talking to him. Ghosts of deceased family members track him down. Complete stranger poltergeists interrupt his soccer try-outs with embarrassing messages for loved ones. And would it be too much to ask for a little respect from the upper classmen? But when his missing best friend shows up in full ghost-mode and claims that the school Principal murdered him, Bradley is plunged into a new level of high school hell.

Now his sister thinks he's gone off the deep end, the Principal is on to him and a group of angry ghosts threaten to trap him on the Other Side unless he locates a stolen heirloom stashed away in the school's infamous lost-and-found. Soon he's sneaking into the high school after hours, stealing priceless artifacts and trying to stay one step ahead of the Principal.

112

To make matters worse, he's finally met an alive girl willing to talk to him – only she might not be so interested when she finds out her undead relative is feeding him all her secrets. Bradley needs to figure out how to preserve his new relationship and retrieve the ancient heirloom before the Principal catches up to him or the angry mob of ghosts trap him forever on the Other Side. Otherwise, he can say goodbye to the land of the living, any semblance of teenage normalcy and any chance of getting a first kiss from the girl of his dreams.

Per your submission guidelines, I have included the first five pages. The full manuscript is available upon request.

Thank you for your time and consideration.

Sincerely,

Samantha Jones

SamanthaJones@querymail.com
111-111-1111

Query Deconstructed

There you have it – an example of a successful, compelling query letter written in less than an hour.

That's the power of swipe files. Most of the work is already done for you. You just fill in the blanks.

If you haven't already done so, I encourage you to compare the Query Template #1 with the fully developed query letter. Note how easy it is to craft mouth-watering paragraphs that propel readers through your letter.

Now It's Your Turn!

As an exercise, take one of the template query letters (the ones with all those brackets) and insert your own book details. Most likely, some of the brackets won't make sense for your story – don't worry about that for now: this draft letter is for your eyes only. Still, see what you come up with and how you like it. This kind of practice is fuel for the final query you craft for submission.

After you finish reading the rest of this book, come back to this draft query letter. Find templates throughout the various swipe files that make more sense to your story and insert them into the query. Feel free to add, change, replace, delete or move around any part of your letter until it clicks.

We're almost done. In the next and last chapter, you'll learn my 5-step process for churning out irresistible query letters in record time…

CONCLUSION

I am delighted that you have read all the way through this book. My biggest hope is that this information helps you write the query letter that gets the agent that gets the book deal, that lets you live the life of your dreams.

It's completely possible. It happens every day to writers just like you.

Where do we go from here?

Here, humbly, are my suggestions…

MY 5-STEP PROCESS FOR EASILY CHURNING OUT IRRESISTIBLE QUERY LETTERS EVERY TIME

First, gather the material you need to write your letter (title, genre, word count, character names, comparisons to popular books in your genre, sample chapters, etc.). For agent research, check out www.ManuscriptWishList.com and the associated Twitter hashtag #MSWL, which stands for manuscript wish list. On both the website and Twitter hashtag, literary agents spell out what they are looking for in a query and manuscript. It's a gold mine of agent information to insert into your hook, book details or salutation section.

Second, write your query letter using the swipe files in this book. Either use one of the Full Query Templates or create your own. Revise, edit and tweak until you are happy. Share your query with beta readers for their feedback. Tinker some more. When you read it, if you don't say, "Heck Yes!" keep reworking it until you do. It's either "Heck Yes!" or it's no.

Third, keep first things first: Focus most of your time and energy on the PITCH section of your query letter – it's by far the most important section. Know how to start your pitch.

Here are a few proven ways to start:

- [CHARACTER] is…
- After…
- From the day…
- The last thing…
- When…

Fourth, give yourself options. One of my "secrets" to writing successful query letters is to create several versions of a query letter using a different mix of words, phrases and templates. In each version, I slightly alter the structure, format and pitch. I emphasize different elements of the story – character, conflicts, settings, etc. After I'm done, I compare the letters to see which one I like best. Sometimes it's also helpful to get feedback from beta readers. Usually one letter stands out. I make any final edits to it and move on to the last step.

Fifth, and finally, send out your query letters! Submit. Your query will never be perfect. When it's "Heck Yes!", send it out. Track your submissions by agent, date, manuscript and response time (agents usually respond within a few weeks to several months).

There you have it: my 5-Step Process for Churning Out Irresistible Query Letters every time. Please follow this process for your own letters using the swipe files in this book.

I'd love to know how it goes for you.

Contact me through www.christopherkokoski.com to share your query stories, learn more writing tips and sign up for my newsletter to be among the first to learn of my new book releases.

What About a Synopsis?

Once you start submitting query letters using the swipe files, agents will start requesting material from you. Namely, most will want a synopsis and sample chapters. It's best to have these polished and ready to go before you submit your first query letter. That way, when an agent wants more, you have more to give. A delay can lead to a denial.

A synopsis is basically a fleshed-out version of the pitch section of your query letter. At the time of this publication, here are two good free resources and a cheap book for perfecting the story synopsis:

> **Blog Post:** https://carlywatters.com/2013/11/04/how-to-write-a-book-synopsis/

> **Blog Post:** http://www.marissameyer.com/blogtype/6-steps-for-writing-a-book-synopsis/

> **Book:** How to Write a Sizzling Synopsis: A Step-by-Step System for Enticing New Readers, Selling More Fiction, and Making Your Books Sound Good by Bryan Cohen (affiliate link)

Hopefully, these resources will get you started on writing a synopsis and help you prepare for an eventual request from an agent. If you ever have any issues with the links, you can always run a simple Internet search for "How to Write a Synopsis for a Novel".

BONUSES!

DOWNLOAD YOUR BONUSES NOW

If you are reading the print version or listening to the audio version, please type the following url into your Internet browser:

http://www.subscribepage.com/InsideSwipeFileBook

OTHER BOOKS

Nonfiction

13 Tools to 10X Your Title (FREE) – Download Now!

Agent Magnets: How to Get Literary Agents and Publishers Begging to See Your Work – Coming in late 2017 or early 2018! (Sign up for my WRITING SECRETS newsletter to get it the moment it is released)

How to Get an Agent With Your Very First Query: Advanced Tools and Tactics for Writing a Query Letter that Literary Agents Can't Resist – Coming in 2018! (Sign up for my WRITING SECRETS newsletter to get it the moment it is released)

Fiction

Past Lives: Serial Killer Thriller Series (Book 1) – Get it FREE!

Present Killing: Serial Killer Thriller Series (Book 2)

Wicker Hollow: A Supernatural Thriller with Angels and Demons **(standalone)**

ABOUT THE AUTHOR

Christopher is the author of the QUERY LETTER SWIPE FILE, the thriller series, *Past Lives*, and the standalone novel, *Wicker Hollow*, along with numerous articles, short stories, national training materials and other how-to books for writers. He is currently at work on his next book.

To book him for a speaking engagement, please contact him at www.christopherkokoski.com

Join his free WRITING SECRETS newsletter to unleash your inner bestseller. For print or audio book listeners, subscribe at http://www.subscribepage.com/WritingSecrets.

ONE FINAL REQUEST

If you enjoyed this book, one of the best ways to share it with others is to leave an honest review. The best reviews tend to balance honesty with specific ways a book has helped you. I would truly appreciate your feedback.

Most readers just swing by my Amazon Author Page, click on the Query Letter Swipe File book cover, scroll down to the Reviews section and write a short review. One sentence is perfect!

For those reading the print copy or listening to the audiobook, please type the following url into your preferred Internet browser: http://amzn.to/2tqLjsE, or simply log onto Amazon.com and search for "Christopher Kokoski".

Thank you!

Christopher

63629539R00076

Made in the USA
Middletown, DE
02 February 2018